To My

Dearest Cherri

Happy Birthday

5/23/01

Love

Mom

Children's
FIRST
Book of
ANIMALS

Children's
FIRST
Book of

ANIMALS

DP
DEMPSEY
PARR

Author and Editor
Neil Morris

Projects created by
Ting Morris

Art Direction
Full Steam Ahead Ltd

Designer
Branka Surla

Project Management
Rosie Alexander

Artwork commissioned by
Branka Surla

Picture Research
Rosie Alexander, Kate Miles, Elaine Willis, Yannick Yago

Editorial Assistant
Lynne French

Additional editorial help from
Hilary Bird, Paul Kilgour, Jenny Sharman

Editorial Director
Jim Miles

The publishers would like to thank the following people for their help:
Suzanne Airey, Jenni Cozens, Pat Crisp

This is a Dempsey Parr Book
This edition published in 2000

Dempsey Parr is an imprint of Parragon

Parragon
Queen Street House,
4 Queen Street,
Bath BA1 1HE, UK

Copyright © Parragon 1998

2 4 6 8 10 9 7 5 3 1

Produced by Miles Kelly Publishing Ltd
Unit 11, Bardfield Centre, Great Bardfield, Essex CM7 4SL

ISBN 1-84084-789-1

Printed in Dubai, U.A.E.

Contents

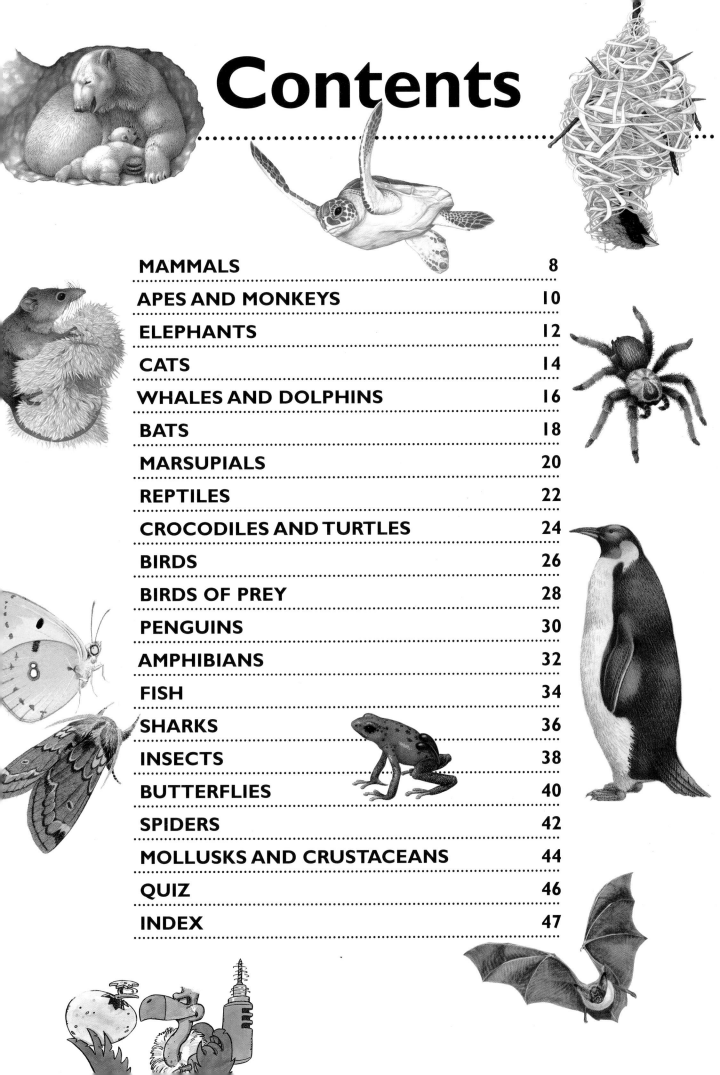

How to use this book

I n this book, every page is filled with information on the sort of topics that you will enjoy reading about.

Information is given in photographs and illustrations, as well as in words. All the pictures are explained by captions, to tell you what you are looking at, and to give even more detailed facts.

Illustrations are clear and simple, and sometimes they are cut away so that you can see inside things. The triangle at the beginning of the caption text points to the illustration concerned.

Beautiful photographs have been specially chosen to bring each subject to life. The caption triangle points to the right photograph.

A New Words box appears on every double-page spread. This list explains some difficult words and technical terms.

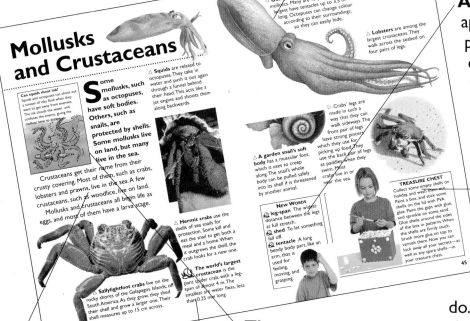

Mollusks and Crustaceans

Can squids shoot ink!
Squids and octopuses can shoot out a stream of inky fluid when they want to get away from enemies. The ink clouds the water, and confuses the enemy, giving the mollusc time to escape.

S ome mollusks, such as octopuses, have soft bodies. Others, such as snails, are protected by shells. Some mollusks live on land, but many live in the sea.

Crustaceans get their name from their crusty covering. Most of them, such as crabs, lobsters and prawns, live in the sea. A few crustaceans, such as woodlice, live on land. Mollusks and crustaceans all begin life as eggs, and most of them have a larva stage.

△ **Squids** are related to octopuses. They take in water and push it out again through a funnel behind their head. This acts like a jet engine and shoots them along backwards.

◁ **Octopuses** are eight-armed mollusks. Many are very small, but the largest have tentacles up to 3.5 m long. Octopuses can change colour according to their surroundings, so they can easily hide.

◁ **Lobsters** are among the largest crustaceans. They walk across the seabed on four pairs of legs.

△ **A garden snail's soft body** has a muscular foot, which it uses to creep along. The snail's whole body can be pulled safely into its shell if is threatened by another animal.

▷ **Crabs' legs** are made in such a way that they can walk sideways. The front pair of legs have strong pincers, which they use for picking up food. They use the back pair of legs as paddles when they swim. Most crabs live in or near the sea.

△ **Hermit crabs** use the shells of sea snails for protection. Some kill and eat the snail to get both a meal and a home. When it outgrows the shell, the crab looks for a new one.

The world's largest crustacean is the giant spider crab, with a leg-span of almost 4 m. The smallest are water fleas, less than 0.25 mm long.

△ **Sallylightfoot crabs** live on the rocky shores of the Galapagos Islands, off South America. As they grow, they shed their shell and grow a larger one. Their shell measures up to 15 cm across.

NEW WORDS
leg-span The widest distance between the legs at full stretch.
shed To let something fall off.
tentacle A long bendy body part, like an arm, that is used for feeling, moving, and grasping.

TREASURE CHEST
Collect some empty shells on holiday, and wash them out. Paint a box, and stick some shells on the lid with PVA glue. Paint the gaps with glue, and sprinkle on some sand. Glue shells around the sides of the box in patterns. When the shells are firmly stuck, brush more glue on top to varnish them. Now you can lock away all your secrets—as well as any spare shells—in your treasure chest.

44

45

Project boxes describe craft activities related to the topic. These are things to make or simple experiments to do. The photograph helps to show you what to do, and is there to inspire you to have a go! But remember, some of the activities can be quite messy, so put old newspaper down first. Always use round-ended scissors, and ask an adult for help if you are unsure of something or need sharp tools or materials.

The main text on each double-page spread gives a short introduction to that particular topic. Every time you turn the page, you will find a new topic.

The cartoons throughout the book are not always meant to be taken too seriously! They are supposed to be fun, but the text that goes with them gives real information.

Captions beginning with a symbol give extra pieces of information that you will find interesting.

Animals

The wildlife kingdom is full of all sorts of amazing animals—mammals, reptiles, birds, amphibians, fish, insects, mollusks, and crustaceans. They live in all parts of the world, in different habitats, and with different life-cycles, and behaviour. There is a lot to learn about them, and there are things we can learn from them.

Which mammals can fly? What is a marsupial? Where do penguins live? These, and hundreds more questions, have fascinating answers, telling us more about the creatures with which we share our planet. We can also learn to respect, and look after, those animals that are threatened by the way humans live.

Mammals

There are many animals in the group we call mammals. Human beings are mammals, too. A mammal has hair or fur on its body, to help keep it warm. Baby mammals are fed with milk from their mother's body.

Mammals live all over the world, from the freezing polar regions to the hot tropics. Most mammals live on land, but whales live in the sea and bats can fly. They are known as warm-blooded animals.

△ **There are more than 400** different breeds of sheep. We shear them so that we can use their furry coats to make wool.

◁ **A porcupine** has long spines, called quills. It can raise and rattle its quills to warn off any of its enemies.

△ **Some mammals,** such as this otter, have whiskers. These help them feel things and find their way about.

◁ **Bears** are large mammals with powerful legs and strong claws. They eat plants as well as meat. They live mainly on the ground but can stand on their back legs and can even climb trees.

The largest mammal is the blue whale. The largest on land is the African elephant. The tallest is the giraffe. The fastest is the cheetah. And the smallest is the tiny hog-nosed bat.

▷ **The white rhinoceros** is one of the world's five species of rhino. They all have horns and for this reason are under threat from hunters.

△ **Kudu antelopes** have beautifully curved horns. Males sometimes use these to fight each other. Kudus live in small groups in Africa, and their main enemies are leopards, lions, and wild dogs.

△ **Farmyard pigs** are descendants of wild boars. Farmers keep them for their meat, which we call pork, ham and bacon. The female pig, called a sow, lies down to feed milk to all her piglets at the same time.

SNOWED IN

Female polar bears dig a den in a snowdrift in the freezing Arctic region. There they give birth to their cubs in midwinter, protecting them from the severe cold and wind. The tiny cubs stay in the den for about three months. Their mother feeds them with her own milk, though she eats nothing herself. Mother and cubs come out onto the snow and ice in spring. Mother then spends most of her time looking for food, such as seals.

Apes and Monkeys

Apes are generally larger than monkeys, and they have no tails. There are four types of ape. Gorillas and chimpanzees live only in Africa, and orangutans and gibbons live only in Southeast Asia.

Many different types of old world monkeys are found in both Africa and Asia. The new world monkeys of Central and South America have long tails, which they often use to hold on to branches as they swing through the trees.

Most apes and monkeys live in the world's rain forests, many of which are being destroyed.

△ **Male mandrills** have very colorful faces. Mandrills live in African forests, staying mainly on the ground in troops of up to 50 animals. They feed on fruit, nuts, and small animals, and sleep in trees.

▷ **Many monkeys**, such as this macaque, live together in large troops. Each troop has a leader, usually an old, strong male. They spend most of their time in trees and have good eyesight, hearing, and sense of smell.

NEW WORDS
grooming Cleaning the skin and fur.
timber Wood that is used for building or making things.
troop An organized group.

▷ **Orangutans** live in the tropical rainforests of Borneo and Sumatra. In the Malay language, this ape's name means "man of the forest." In many places, its home is being cut down for timber. Reserves have been set up to protect it.

▽ **The gorilla** is the largest ape. Males are sometimes over 6 feet (1.8 m) tall, the same height as a tall man. They are powerful, but they are also peaceful and gentle. They rarely climb trees.

△ **Grooming** each other to get rid of irritating pests is an enjoyable group activity for these chimpanzees.

▷ **South American spider monkeys** have amazing tails which can wrap round and cling to branches.

 **Chimpanzees** are good tool-makers. They use sticks to get honey and insects from nests, and they use stones to crack nuts.

MONKEY MOBILE
Trace the monkey (right) and cut out its shape. Draw around the shape on cardboard and cut it out. Make two more monkeys and draw on faces. Make a small hole in each monkey and tie on pieces of thread. Tie the monkeys to some rolled cardboard. When the monkeys are balanced, fix the knots with a drop of glue.

Elephants

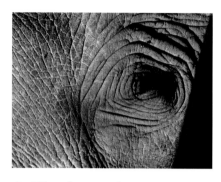

△ **Elephants** have thick, wrinkled skin. Their eyesight is not very good, but they have good hearing and an excellent sense of smell.

▷ **An elephant's tusks** are really two big teeth made of ivory. They are useful for digging and breaking off large branches. The trunk can be used to pick up food and guide it into an elephant's mouth.

▽ **Elephants love bathing.** They can give themselves a shower through their trunks and are good swimmers.

There are two species (or two different kinds), of elephant—African and Asian. The African elephant has large ears and is the world's biggest land animal. Males can grow up to 13 feet (4 m) high at the shoulder, which is over twice as tall as a man. They can weigh up to 7 tons, which is as much as 90 people! Asian elephants are smaller and lighter, with smaller ears. They live in India, Sri Lanka, and parts of Southeast Asia.

△ **A tree** is useful for scratching an annoying itch!

NEW WORDS

herd A large group of animals living together.

logging Cutting down trees to use the wood.

trunk An elephant's long, bendy nose.

tusk One of the two long pointed teeth sticking out of an elephant's mouth.

▷ **Asian elephants** are used in the logging industry, because they can move and carry very heavy loads. Riders sit behind the animal's neck. In some countries, elephants are still used as a means of getting around.

Elephants sometimes use their trunks as snorkels. When they swim, they can stick their trunks upward so that they breathe in plenty of air.

Do elephants use skin care?
Yes! To prevent their skin from cracking, elephants wallow and cover themselves in cool mud. This dries on their bodies and helps protect them from the burning sun. It also gets rid of flies and ticks. An elephant's color depends on the mud it wallows in.

◁ **Elephants** can reach food high up in trees. They are vegetarians, and their diet includes leaves, fruit, bark, and roots.

Elephants live in family groups, which often join together to make large herds. Each group is led by a female elephant, who is usually the oldest. She decides which routes the herd should follow to find food and water, often traveling in single file.

Cats

△ **Cheetahs** are the fastest cats. In fact, they are the fastest runners in the world. They can reach a speed of 60 mph (100 kph) for a short distance.

🐾 **Tigers** are the biggest cats. From head to tail they are up to 12 feet (3.6 m) long. These powerful animals make very good mothers to their baby cubs.

There are a number of species, or different kinds, of cats. Even the biggest wild cats are relatives of our pet cats at home!

All cats are carnivores. They are built to hunt, and their bodies are powerful. To help them catch their prey, cats have sharp eyesight and a good sense of smell. They can run very fast too. Their size, coloring, and coat patterns vary, but all cats have a similar shape.

🐾 **Pet cats** are used to living with people, and to being fed by their owners. But sometimes they hunt, chasing after birds and mice before pouncing. While lions and tigers roar, a pet cat just meows!

jaguar

puma

▷ **Members of the cat family:** they look alike but live in different ways.

▷ **Male and female lions** look very different. The male has a big brown mane. Lions are the only cats that live together in groups, called prides. Lions like to sit around and let the lionesses do most of the hunting.

◁ **The top male** lion is challenged by other males in the pride from time to time. He has to fight them in order to keep his position as the dominant male in the group.

△ **Big cats** like flat, open country, where they can see a long way. They follow their prey until they are close enough to strike.

▷ **Pet cats** and many of the big cats don't like water. But tigers search it out during the hottest part of the day. Then they are often found cooling off in a pool. They are excellent swimmers and can easily cross rivers.

Why do leopards have spots?
Because they make leopards difficult to see. From a distance, the black spots on the yellow fur look like light on the grass or in the trees. This is called camouflage. It helps the leopard to hide from the animals it is hunting, and from those hunting it.

NEW WORDS
🐾 **carnivore** An animal that eats meat.
🐾 **coat** The fur on an animal.
🐾 **mane** Long, thick hair growing around a male lion's neck. Horses have manes too.
🐾 **prey** An animal hunted by another for food.
🐾 **pride** A group of lions, lionesses and cubs that live together.
🐾 **dominant** To be the most important animal, or the leader, among a group of animals.

leopard

lynx

black panther

cheetah

lions

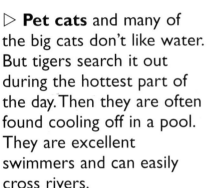

WHALES TO SCALE

Draw whales and dolphins in scale with each other. You can use the scale 1:144. This means using an inch for every 12 feet, so your blue whale will be 9 inches long. The whales' real lengths are: common dolphin 6 feet, bottlenose dolphin 12 feet, narwhal 20 feet, pilot whale 25 feet, killer whale 30 feet, and the blue whale 108 feet.

△ **Pilot whales**, like the one at the top of the photo, have a big, round head. They live in large groups, called schools, of hundreds or even thousands. The other dolphin is a bottlenose.

NEW WORDS

baleen The whalebone at the front of some whales' mouths.

blowhole The nostril on top of a whale's head, through which it breathes.

dolphinarium A pool for dolphins, where they give public displays.

school A group of fish, whales, or dolphins.

▽ **The blue whale** is the largest animal in the world. It can grow up to 108 feet (33 m) long and weigh over 150 tons. Blue whales swim in all the world's oceans, usually alone or in small groups.

△ **These common dolphins** are leaping out of the water at great speed. Most dolphins swim at about 20 mph (30 kph). This is over three times faster than even the quickest human swimmers can manage.

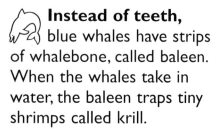

Instead of teeth, blue whales have strips of whalebone, called baleen. When the whales take in water, the baleen traps tiny shrimps called krill.

Other whales, such as killer whales and sperm whales, have teeth. Dolphins are small-toothed whales.

Whales and Dolphins

△ **The narwhal** is a small Arctic whale with a long tusk.

Whales and dolphins are mammals, and they cannot breathe underwater like fish. So they come to the surface often, to take in air. Whales and dolphins breathe in and out through a blowhole on the top of the head. When they let out used air, they usually send out a spray of water at the same time.

△ **Some whales and dolphins** are kept in zoos and dolphinariums. Killer whales are very popular performers. They can jump as high as 16 feet (5 m).

▷ **Many whales and dolphins** live and hunt for their food in groups. They eat fish, squid, and shrimps.

blue whale

17

Bats

Bats are different from all other mammals in one way: they can fly. They do not have feathery wings like birds but, instead, have double layers of skin stretched over thin bones.

There are nearly a thousand different kinds of bats. Most are nocturnal, which means that they are active only at night. They sleep during the day and come out at night to find food. Most bats live on insects alone, but some eat fruit and nectar and others even hunt small animals. Bats live in almost every part of the world, except in the cold polar regions.

△ **All bats** have large, sensitive ears to steer by. These help them pick up echoes of the high-pitched sounds they make. Most bats have razor-sharp teeth.

Bats are relatively small creatures with large wings. A vampire bat's body is only about 4 inches (10 cm) long, but it has a wingspan of up to 7 inches (18 cm).

▽ **A bat's long arm** ends in four fingers and a strong, hook-shaped thumb. When its wings are folded, the bat can use its thumbs to climb trees or rocks.

In a cave in Texas, 20 million free-tailed bats were found in one single colony.

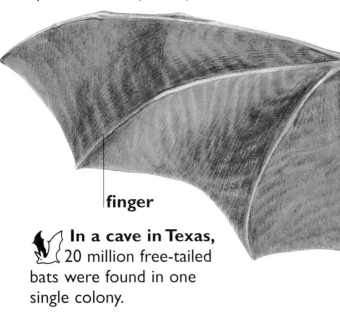

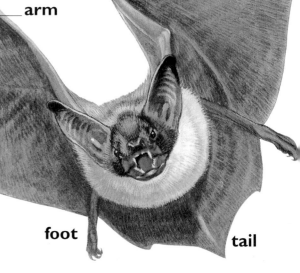

thumb

arm

finger

foot

tail

▷ **Bats hang upside down** by their feet when they rest or sleep. They often live in caves, where there may be thousands of bats crowded together on the walls and ceiling. Smaller bat colonies of up to 12 bats may live together inside a hollow tree.

△ **Bats use echoes** from their high-pitched squeaks to catch insects. The echoes help the bats make up a sound picture of what is around them. They do not need to use their eyes so much, but it is not true that they are "as blind as a bat."

▽ **Three different bat faces.** The vampire bat lives in Central and South America. It uses its sharp teeth and tubelike tongue to suck animals' blood.

Do bats fish?
Some bats really do fish, in the same way that some birds do. The fisherman (or bulldog) bat of Mexico lives near mangrove swamps. When it hunts, it swoops down near the water. Then the bat dips quickly into the water with its clawlike feet, catches a small fish and scoops it up into its mouth.

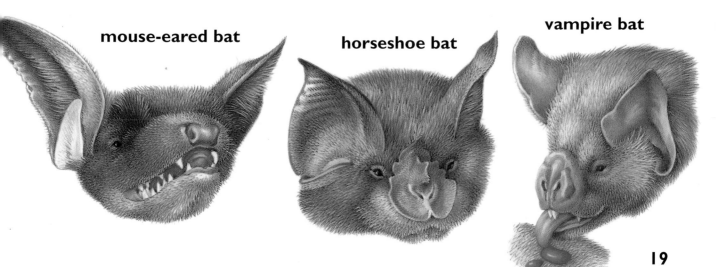

mouse-eared bat

horseshoe bat

vampire bat

19

Marsupials

Marsupials are a special group of mammals. Unlike all other animals, female marsupials have a pouch. They give birth to tiny babies, who stay in the pouch and live off their mother's milk until they are big enough to venture into the outside world. The soft pouch is warm and snug.

Most marsupials, like kangaroos, koalas, and wombats, live in Australia. Some smaller kinds, called opossums, live in North and South America.

△ **Wallabies** are like small kangaroos. This unusual wallaby is called an albino—it has white fur and pink eyes. Most wallabies are gray or brown.

NEW WORDS
albino An animal that has very little color in its skin, hair, and eyes.
joey A baby kangaroo.
marsupial A type of mammal in which the female has a pouch.

▽ **Baby kangaroos** are called joeys. When they are old enough to leave the pouch, they jump back in if there is danger. They turn around inside the pouch and poke their heads out.

jumping in

turning around

Do kangaroos box?
Sometimes male kangaroos, called bucks, try out their strength against each other. Standing on their hind, (or back,) legs, they hit out with their arms, which looks like boxing. They also rest on their tails and kick out with their hind legs, which does more damage.

▽ **The tiny honey possum** feeds on pollen and nectar. Its 4 inch (10 cm) tail, which it uses for gripping like some monkeys, is longer than its body.

◁ **A female kangaroo** and her joey. Joeys have an easy time, sitting in the pouch while their mother finds food. Kangaroos hop on their huge back legs and can travel more than 30 feet (9 m) in one giant leap.

△ **Koalas** are expert climbers. They spend most of their time near the top of eucalyptus trees, eating the tender shoots. Although they look like small bears, koalas have nothing to do with the bear family.

ROO RACERS
Draw two kangaroos on cardboard and cut them out. Make a hole just below the head and run some string through. Tie one end of each length of string to a chair leg and lie the racers on their backs a couple of yards away. Then you and a friend can race your kangaroos by pulling on the string and then letting it go. The chair is the finishing line.

Reptiles

Snakes, lizards, and crocodiles are all reptiles. Unlike mammals, these scaly skinned animals are all cold-blooded. This means that they always need lots of sunshine to warm them up.

△ **Marine iguanas** are the only lizards that swim in the sea. They live around the Galapagos Islands, in the Pacific Ocean. They go to sea to feed on seaweed and then warm up on the islands' volcanic rocks.

The largest lizard is the Komodo dragon of Indonesia. It can grow up to 10 feet (3 m) long.

▽ **The horned lizard** has strong armour, to protect it from its enemies. It has pointed scales, as well as horns behind its head. It lives in dry areas and deserts of America, where it feeds mainly on ants. The female horned lizard lays her eggs in a hole in the ground.

A skink is a kind of lizard. It can make its tail fall off if when it is attacked by an enemy. This usually confuses the enemy, so that the lizard can quickly escape. It then grows a new tail.

Reptiles are found on land and in water. Most live in warm parts of the world, and some live in hot deserts. They move into a burrow if it is too hot above ground, or if it is ever too cold in winter.

Most reptiles have four legs, but snakes are long, legless reptiles. All snakes are meat-eaters, and some kill their prey with poison from hollow teeth called fangs.

NEW WORDS

chameleon A lizard with a long tongue and the ability to change color.

fang A snake's long, pointed, hollow tooth, through which it can pass its poison.

marine Living in, or from, the sea.

▷ **Chameleons** are slow-moving, tree-living lizards. If they see an insect within range, they shoot out a long sticky tongue to catch it. They can also change color to suit their surroundings or their mood. An angry chameleon may turn black.

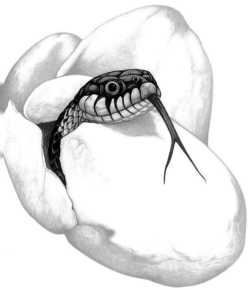

△ **Most reptiles lay eggs**, which are soft and leathery. Snakes lay their eggs in shallow holes and cover them with a thin layer of soil. When the baby snakes hatch out, they have to look after themselves.

The longest snake is the reticulated python of Southeast Asia, which grows up to 30 feet (9 m) long. The most poisonous snake is the small-scaled snake living in Australia.

▽ **Emerald tree boas** live in the rain forests of South America. They wrap themselves around branches and watch out for prey, often birds and bats. They move fast and also swim very well.

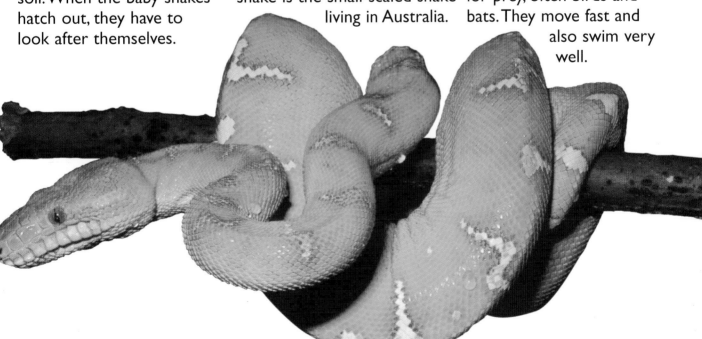

Crocodiles and Turtles

Crocodiles and alligators belong to a group of reptiles called crocodilians. They are large, powerful animals with long tails and strong jaws. Crocodilians live in or close to water and are found mainly in rivers in hot countries.

Turtles and tortoises have a hard shell made of bony plates. Turtles move slowly on land but are very good, fast swimmers. Tortoises however, spend all their time on land.

△ **American alligators** live in rivers and swamps of southeastern USA. They can grow more than 15 feet (4.5 m) long and eat fish, small mammals and birds.

▽ **The hawksbill turtle** is found near the rocky coasts and coral reefs of our oceans. The females lay about 150 eggs at a time.

During a long period of hot, dry weather, crocodiles may bury themselves deep in the mud and go to sleep. They will stay there until the weather changes.

▽ **Green turtles** spend most of their time at sea, only coming on land to sleep and to lay eggs. At nesting time they travel hundreds or even thousands of miles to lay eggs on the beach where they were born.

◁ **The gavial** is a type of crocodilian with a long, thin snout. It has about 100 sharp teeth, which it uses to catch fish and frogs. Gavials can be found in the big rivers of Malaysia and northern India.

MAKE A JUNK CROC

Crunch sheets of newspaper up into different-sized balls and arrange them into a crocodile shape. Make two jaws and four legs, and then tape everything together. Mix some wallpaper paste and stick thin strips of newspaper all over the crocodile with the paste. Stick on three layers, and then leave it to dry. Add some jagged cardboard teeth, two eyes, and paint the croc green all over.

▷ **Female American alligators** and African crocodiles are caring mothers. When their babies have hatched, they carry them to a nearby pool in their mouths.

▽ **Giant tortoises** on the Galapagos Islands grow up to 54 inches (135 cm) long.

NEW WORDS

crocodilian Any one of a group of large reptiles that includes crocodiles and alligators.

reef A row of underwater rocks.

tortoise A large, slow-moving land turtle.

Birds

Birds are the only animals with feathers. They have wings, and most are expert fliers. There are more than 9,000 different kinds, living in all parts of the world.

Female birds lay eggs, and most build nests to protect them. When the eggs hatch out, the adults feed their young until the small birds can fly and leave the nest.

△ **Gulls** and other seabirds spend much of their time at sea. They glide over the water, waiting to swoop down to catch fish. Many seabirds nest on rocky cliffs.

▽ **Arctic terns** raise their young near the North Pole. Then they fly south to the Antarctic for the summer. In the autumn they fly north again, making a round trip of 21,000 miles (36,000 km).

◁ **The Indian peacock** spreads his tail feathers into a fan. He does this to attract the female peahen.

▽ **Birds** have various beaks. With its beak, a macaw can crack nuts, a pelican scoops fish, and an eagle can tear meat.

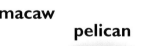
macaw

pelican

flamingo

DIFFERENT NESTS

horned grebe

barn swallow

osprey

ovenbird

weaver bird

willow flycatcher

bird of
paradise

BIRD OF PARADISE

Draw a bird of paradise on blue cardboard with white crayon. Cut out pieces of colored paper to fit the head and body, and stick feather shapes on the body. Add long strips of tissue paper for the tail, and don't forget feet, a beak and a button eye. You could make a rain forest background too, with real twigs and leaves.

toucan

bald eagle

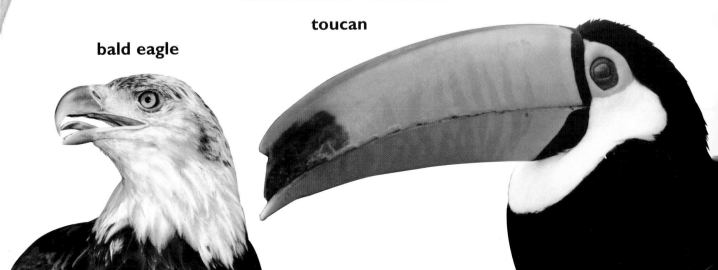

Birds of Prey

Birds that hunt animals for food are called birds of prey. Eagles, hawks, and falcons all have hooked beaks and strong, sharp talons.

They are fast fliers and have excellent long-distance eyesight. They can swoop down on their prey from a great height.

Most owls hunt at night and they can fly with hardly a sound. Their feathers have a soft fringe, to muffle the sound of their wings.

Vultures are scavengers. Other animals make a kill for them and then they eat the leftovers.

△ **The bald eagle** gets its name from its white head feathers. Bald eagles feed on fish, waterbirds, and rabbits. They live along coasts, rivers, and lakes in North America.

▷ **The osprey**, or fish-hawk, is found in most parts of the world. It is an excellent catcher of fish. The osprey circles over the water and then plunges in, feet forward, to snatch the fish in its talons. Sometimes the osprey dives right under the water to get the fish.

NEW WORDS
marrow The soft substance inside bones.
scavenger An animal that looks for and lives off scraps of dead meat killed by others.
talon A strong claw.

28

◁ **White-backed vultures** find plenty of food on the African grasslands. They wait for the big cats to have their meal first. After their own meal, vultures clean their feathers well, so that they are always in good flying condition.

talons

Which birds use tools?
Egyptian vultures use stones as tools. They like to eat ostrich eggs, which are too big and tough to crack open with their beak. So the vultures pick up stones and drop them on the eggs to crack them. Then they feed on the insides.

△ **The lammergeier,** or bearded vulture, picks up bones and drops them onto rocks, to get at the marrow inside.

The peregrine falcon is the world's fastest bird. It can travel over 200 mph (350 kph) as it dives towards its prey. It eats other birds, especially pigeons.

The condor of the Andes mountains in South America is the world's biggest bird of prey. Weighing up to 30 pounds, it can soar for long distances on its enormous wings. The condor has a wingspan of 10 feet (3 m) and flies at a height of up to 23,000 feet (7,000 m).

△ **Owls** have many advantages as night hunters. Their round face helps funnel sounds to their ear openings, which lie under feathered flaps. They can also turn their head right around, to see behind them with their large eyes.

29

△ **Rockhopper penguins** have long yellow or orange feathers above their eyes. They often nest on clifftops, using pebbles or grass. They reach their colony by hopping from rock to rock, as their name suggests.

△ **After a winter at sea,** Snares Island penguins arrive at the islands of the same name, south of New Zealand. They return to these islands every August to breed again.

▽ **These Adélie penguins** are waddling about on an iceberg, off the coast of Antarctica. To climb out of the sea, penguins first dive down and then shoot out of the water at great speed, landing on their feet. To get back into the sea, they simply jump in.

◁ **Penguins** feed mainly on fish, squid and small shrimplike krill. They dive deep underwater, using their feet as rudders, and come to the surface regularly to breathe. Gentoo penguins can swim at up to 16 mph (27 kph).

Penguins

Like all the world's birds, penguins are covered with feathers. But penguin feathers are short and thick. They are waterproof, and keep the animals warm in cold seas.

Penguins have a horny beak for catching food. They also have a small pair of wings, but nevertheless, can't fly. They use their wings as flippers. These birds spend most of their time at sea and are fast, skilful swimmers.

There are 18 different kinds of penguin, and they all live near the coasts of the cold southern oceans. Many live in the frozen region of Antarctica.

emperor penguin

little blue penguin

▷ **The smallest penguins** are "little blues" standing 16 inches (40 cm) high. Emperor penguins are the biggest at 48 inches (120 cm) tall.

△ **Antarctic emperor penguins** keep their eggs and chicks on their feet, for warmth. It is the male bird who does this job, while the female feeds her young.

NEW WORDS
chick A baby bird, such as a young penguin.
krill Tiny shrimplike creatures that are eaten by penguins and whales.

A PENGUIN PLAYMATE
Pour sand into an empty plastic bottle and tape a washball to the top. Tape a cardboard beak to the head. Mix wallpaper paste and paste thin strips of newspaper over the penguin. When it's dry, paint the penguin white. Leave to dry again before painting the head, back and flippers black, leaving white circles for the eyes. You could use your penguin as a bookend.

Amphibians

Frogs, toads, newts, and salamanders belong to a group of animals called amphibians. They spend part of their lives on land and part in water, but amphibians don't live in the sea.

Amphibians go back to water when it is time to lay their eggs. Females may lay their eggs in or near a pond or stream. Most frogs and toads lay between 1,000 and 20,000 eggs. These large clusters of eggs are called spawn.

△ **Tree frogs** have round suckers at the end of their toes. These help them to grip trunks, branches, and even shiny leaves.

▷ **Large North American bullfrogs** can grow up to 8 inches (20 cm) long. This bullfrog has caught an earthworm, but they eat much larger prey too. A big bullfrog might catch a mouse or even a small snake.

frogs eggs or spawn

froglet with legs

FROG LIFE CYCLE
A frog's eggs hatch into tadpoles in the water. The tadpoles grow legs and turn into froglets. Finally the young frogs can leave the water and hop out onto land.

swimming tadpole

young frog

◁ **This smooth-skinned giant salamander** lives in the rivers, lakes, and cool, damp forests of western USA. It can grow to 12 inches (30 cm) long. Most salamanders are silent, but this one can make a low-pitched cry.

What are mouth-brooders?
A male mouth-brooding frog can gather up to 15 eggs with its tongue and put them in its mouth. But it doesn't eat the eggs. It keeps them in its vocal sac to turn into tadpoles. When the froglets are ready, they jump out.

▷ **Arrow-poison frogs** of South America are very poisonous. Females lay up to six eggs on land. When they hatch, the male carries the tadpoles on his back to a tree hole filled with water or to a water plant, so that they can begin life in water.

Toads usually have a rougher, bumpier skin than frogs which is often covered with warts. Toads usually live in drier places. They have wider bodies and shorter, less powerful legs, which means that they are not such good jumpers.

NEW WORDS
froglet A young frog that develops from a tadpole.
spawn The mass of eggs produced by amphibians.
tadpole The young frog or toad that develops from an egg and lives in water.
vocal sac Loose folds of skin in male frogs that can fill with air to make a noise.

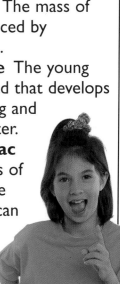

△ **Frogs** have long back legs. These are good for swimming and we copy their action when we swim breaststroke. These powerful legs are also useful for jumping on land. Common frogs can leap about 2 feet (60 cm), and South African sharp-nosed frogs can jump over 10 feet (3 m)!

Female surinam toads keep their eggs in holes in their skin. The young toads develop in these holes.

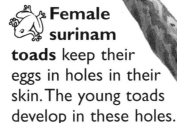

Fish

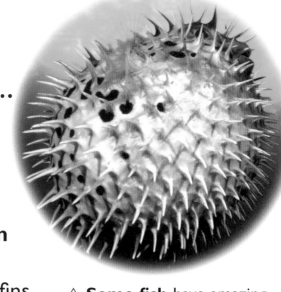

There are more than 20,000 different kinds of fish in the world's oceans, lakes, and rivers. Like other animals, fish live in warm parts of the world, as well as in cold polar seas.

Many fish have streamlined bodies and fins, to help them swim. They have gills instead of lungs, so that they can breathe under water.

Fish have the same body temperature as the waters in which they live and swim.

△ **Some fish** have amazing defences. This porcupine fish has swollen up into a spiny ball. It must have sensed danger nearby.

▽ **Salmon** have to work very hard to make their way upriver from the ocean to breed. They swim against the current of the river and leap over the shallow, rocky parts.

◁ **The butterfly fish** has beautiful colors and strong contrasting markings.

▽ **The lionfish** has fins sticking out all over its body, and a row of poisonous spines. It grows up to 15 inches (38 cm) long.

NEW WORDS
breed To produce babies.
fin A thin flat part that sticks out of a fish's body and helps it to swim.
gill The parts of their bodies through which fishes breathe.
streamlined Shaped smoothly for moving faster.

▽ **The ray** has a flat body, which helps it glide along the bottom of the sea. Rays feed mainly on shellfish, which they crack open with their strong teeth. Some kinds of rays can sting with their tails.

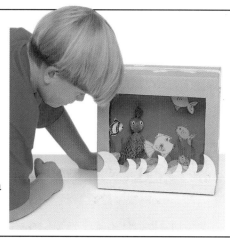

HOW FISH BREATHE

1. A fish takes in water through its mouth.

2. The water flows over its gills and oxygen passes into its bloodstream.

gills

3. The water is then pushed back out through the gill covers.

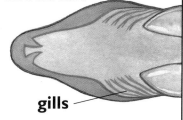

gill covers

▷ **Seahorses** look very strange. They swim in an upright position and live near seaweed, which they can hold on to with their tails. Seahorses are a fish which can change color.

▷ **This trumpet fish** is long and thin, growing up to 3 feet (0.9 m) long. Its eyes are set well back from its jaws. Compare its shape to the ray and the porcupine fish.

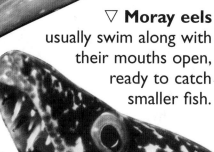

▽ **Moray eels** usually swim along with their mouths open, ready to catch smaller fish.

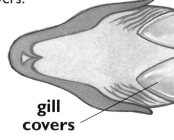

Electric eels kill fish and other sea animals with electric shocks from their tail. These big South American fish are up to 6 feet (1.8 m) long.

Sharks

Sharks are the fierce hunters of the world's oceans. People are very frightened of them, though many sharks are quite harmless.

Most fish have an air bag, called a swim bladder, which helps to keep them afloat. Sharks don't have a swim bladder, which means they have to keep swimming all the time, or else they would sink to the bottom. Sharks are different from most other fish in another way too. A shark's skeleton is made of rubbery cartilage instead of bone.

△ Some sharks lay eggs rather than giving birth to live babies. They lay their eggs in a tough case, which we call a mermaid's purse. The baby fish grow inside the case, which attaches itself to weeds.

△ **The great white shark** is the most famous of all the sharks. It grows up to 20 feet (6 m) long, or more.

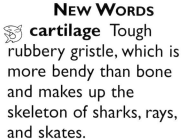

△ **Shark's teeth** form double or triple rows and are set inside a tooth bed. New teeth are formed in grooves in this area every 1-2 weeks to replace old or worn-out teeth.

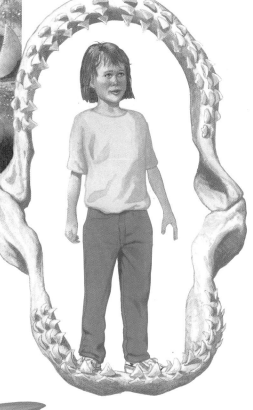

nurse shark

🦈 **The whale shark** is the world's largest fish, growing over 40 feet (12 m) long. But this shark is not dangerous. It uses its huge mouth as a scoop for catching and eating tiny sea creatures. The smallest shark is the dwarf shark at just 6 inches (15 cm) long.

tiger shark

△ **Tiger sharks** are thought to be dangerous to people, but any shark will only attack if it smells blood. All sharks have an excellent sense of smell and good hearing, helping them hunt at night.

▷ **Reef sharks** live near coral reefs, where there are plenty of smaller fish and other sea creatures for them to feed on.

Insects

head

antennae

thorax

abdomen

△ **This wasp** shows the three basic body parts of an insect—a head, a thorax, and an abdomen. Its legs and wings are attached to the thorax, and its antennae to the head.

▽ **This honey bee** is collecting nectar and pollen from a flower. The bee will take the food to its nest, where it will be stored as honey.

nsects are tiny animals that are found all over the world—from scorching deserts to steaming rain forests and icy lakes.

Insects have no backbone, and they are protected by a hard, outer skeleton or shell. Because they are so small, they can fit into tiny places and don't need much food to live on. They all have six legs, and most have wings and can fly. Many insects have two pairs of wings, but flies have just one pair.

termite mound

food stores

queen's chamber

tunnel

egg chambers

▷ **Termites** live in colonies and build huge mounds as nests. Each colony is ruled by a king and a queen. Soldier termites defend the nest, and most of the termites are workers.

◁ **Ladybugs** are a kind of beetle. They feed on much smaller insects, called aphids and scale insects, which they find on plants. The ladybug's hard, outer wings protect the flying wings underneath.

▷ **Female mosquitoes** are bloodsuckers. They insert a needle-like tube into birds and mammals, including humans, and suck up a tiny amount of blood.

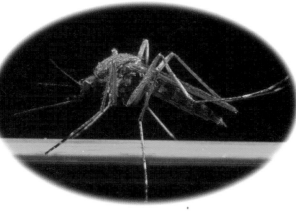

Why do wasps sting?
Wasps—and bees—mainly sting to defend themselves and their nests. Wasps also use their sting to stun or kill other insects. The sting is really a tiny tube. When it is hooked in place, the insect pumps poison down the tube.

△ **Beetles** live just about everywhere on Earth. Some live in water, and many can fly. This horned beetle is found in Borneo, in Southeast Asia.

🐝 **A single bee** would have to visit more than 4,000 flowers to make one tablespoon of honey. A large beehive may contain 60,000 worker bees.

NEW WORDS
🐝 **abdomen** The lower or back part of an insect's body.
🐝 **antennae** An insect's very sensitive feelers, attached to its head.
🐝 **aphid** A tiny insect that feeds on plants.
🐝 **termite** Also called a white ant, this insect lives in a colony.
🐝 **thorax** The upper or front part of an insect's body, to which its wings and legs are attached.

Butterflies

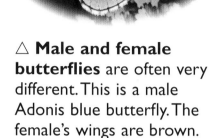

Butterflies have thin, delicate wings, covered with tiny overlapping scales. These give butterflies their wonderful colors.

Like many insects, butterflies change their bodies as they develop. This change is called metamorphosis. Eggs develop into caterpillars. Each caterpillar turns into a chrysalis, and the final stage is a beautiful butterfly.

Butterflies are usually bright-colored and fly during the day. Most moths have much duller colors and are night-fliers.

△ **Male and female butterflies** are often very different. This is a male Adonis blue butterfly. The female's wings are brown.

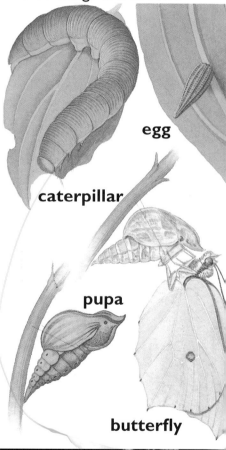

egg

caterpillar

pupa

butterfly

△ **This peacock butterfly** has eyespots on its wings. These may be there to confuse or frighten a bird that might otherwise attack the insect.

▷ **A caterpillar** hatches from a butterfly egg. The caterpillar becomes a pupa, or chrysalis. A butterfly develops inside the pupa, and eventually emerges.

▷ **A hawkmoth caterpillar.** In other insects, this stage is called a larva. We call small insect larvae grubs or maggots.

The world's largest butterfly is the Queen Alexandra's birdwing, with a wingspan of more than 11 inches (28 cm).

40

NEW WORDS

🦋 **larva** The worm like stage of butterflies or insects after hatching.

🦋 **caterpillar** The larva of butterflies and moths.

🦋 **metamorphosis** The way insects change.

🦋 **pupa** The next stage after being a larva.

🦋 **chrysalis** A butterfly or moth pupa.

▷ **Some butterflies** and moths will travel huge distances. Often thousands and even millions of butterflies travel together. Some can even cross the Atlantic Ocean.

◁ **Unlike most moths,** the emperor moth flies by day. Females give off a strong scent, which males can pick up half a mile away.

△ **Butterflies** live almost everywhere in the world. These are found in India. Butterflies have a very keen sense of smell. They mainly use their antennae to smell, but some smell through "noses" on their feet.

BUTTERFLY OR MOTH?
When a butterfly rests, it holds its wings up. A moth folds its wings flat.

▽ **Hawkmoths** feed on nectar. They get this from flowers through their long tube-shaped tongues. Hawkmoths have large bodies and are fast fliers.

BUTTERFLY PRINTS
Fold a sheet of paper in half. Open it up and drop blobs of different-colored paints around the crease in the middle of the paper. Fold the two halves over and press the paper down. When you open it again, you will see that you have made a beautiful butterfly. When they are dry, cut your butterflies out and hang them up.

◁ **Scorpions** have a poisonous sting in their tails, which they use to paralyse prey. They also have powerful claws.

▷ **A hunting spider** from Costa Rica in, Central America. But spiders also live in cold parts of the world.

△ **Trapdoor spiders** have a very clever system for catching insects. The spider digs a burrow, lines it with silk and covers the entrance with a trapdoor. Then it lies in wait. When an insect passes nearby, the spider feels the ground move. Then it jumps out and catches the insect, quickly dragging it into its burrow.

△ **Web-making spiders** feel the silk threads of the web move when an insect is caught. They tie their prey up in a band of silk.

◁ **Garden spiders** spin beautiful circular webs. These are easily damaged, and the spiders spend a lot of time repairing them. The webs show up well when the air outside is damp.

Spiders

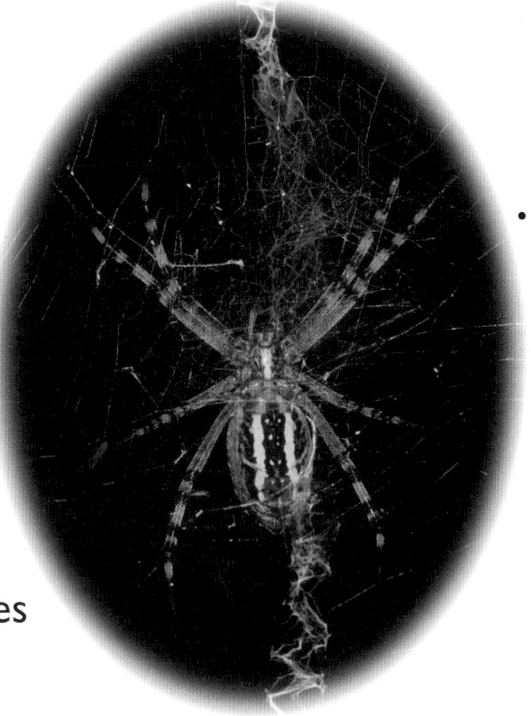

Spiders are similar in some ways to insects, but they belong to a different group of animals called arachnids. Scorpions, ticks, and mites are arachnids too.

Spiders have eight legs, while insects have six. Many spiders spin silky webs to catch flies and other small insects. They have fangs for seizing their prey. Most spiders paralyze their prey with poison before they kill and eat them. But only a few spiders are poisonous to humans.

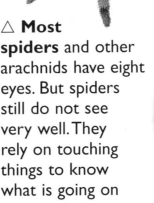

△ **There are about 40,000** different kinds of spider, and there can be many millions of each type. In a grassy meadow, there may be as many as 50 spiders in a square foot.

NEW WORDS

arachnid A group of animals that includes spiders, scorpions, ticks, and mites.
paralyze To make something unable to move.
spiderling A young spider.

△ **Most spiders** and other arachnids have eight eyes. But spiders still do not see very well. They rely on touching things to know what is going on around them.

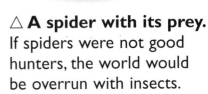

△ **A spider with its prey.** If spiders were not good hunters, the world would be overrun with insects.

◁ **Female spiders** lay up to 2,000 eggs, which they wrap in a bundle of silk threads. Spiderlings hatch from the eggs.

Mollusks and Crustaceans

Can squids shoot ink?
Squids and octopuses can shoot out a stream of inky fluid when they want to get away from enemies. The ink clouds the water and confuses the enemy, giving the mollusk time to escape.

Some mollusks, such as octopuses, have soft bodies. Others, such as snails, are protected by shells. Some mollusks live on land but many live in the sea.

Crustaceans get their name from their crusty covering. Most of them, such as crabs, lobsters, and shrimp, live in the sea. A few crustaceans, such as woodlice, live on land.

Mollusks and crustaceans all begin life as eggs, and most of them have a larva stage.

△ **Squids** are related to octopuses. They take in water and push it out again through a funnel behind their head. This acts like a jet engine and shoots them along backward.

△ **Hermit crabs** use the shells of sea snails for protection. Some kill and eat the snail to get both a meal and a home. When it outgrows the shell, the crab looks for a new one.

The world's largest crustacean is the giant spider crab, which has a legspan of almost 13 feet (4 m).

△ **Sallylightfoot crabs** live on the rocky shores of the Galapagos Islands, off South America. As they grow, they shed their shells and grow bigger ones. These measure up to 6 inches (15 cm) across.

◁ **Octopuses** are eight-armed molluscs. Many are very small, but the largest have tentacles up to 12 feet (3.5 m) long. Octopuses can change color according to their surroundings, so they can easily hide.

△ **Lobsters** are among the largest crustaceans. They walk across the seabed on four pairs of legs.

△ **A garden snail's soft body** has a muscular foot, which it uses to creep along. The snail's whole body can be pulled safely into its shell if it is threatened by another animal.

▷ Crabs' legs are made in such a way that they can walk sideways. The front pair of legs have strong pincers which they use for picking up food. They use the back pair of legs as paddles when they swim. Most crabs live in or near the sea.

NEW WORDS

🐌 **legspan** The widest distance between the legs at full stretch.

🐌 **shed** To let something fall off.

🐌 **tentacle** A long bendy body part, like an arm, that is used for feeling, moving and grasping.

TREASURE CHEST
Collect some empty shells on vacation and wash them out. Paint a box and stick some shells on the lid with glue. Paint the gaps with glue and sprinkle on some sand. Glue shells around the sides of the box in patterns. When the shells are firmly stuck, brush more glue on top to varnish them. Now you can lock away all your secrets—as well as any spare shells—in your treasure chest.

Quiz

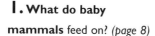

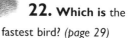

1. **What do baby mammals** feed on? *(page 8)*
2. **Where do polar bears** give birth? *(page 9)*
3. **Can you name** four kinds of apes? *(page 10)*
4. **Where do** orangutans live? *(page 11)*
5. **Which is the world's biggest** land animal? *(page 12)*
6. **What do** elephants eat? *(page 13)*
7. **Which are** the fastest cats? *(page 14)*
8. **Which big cat** likes water? *(page 15)*
9. **How long** is a blue whale? *(page 16)*
10. **What does a narwhal** have on its head? *(page 17)*
11. **What is different about bats,** compared with other mammals? *(page 18)*
12. **What do bats** use to catch insects? *(page 19)*
13. **What is** another name for a baby kangaroo? *(page 20)*
14. **Which trees** do koalas live in? *(page 21)*
15. **Are reptiles warm-blooded** or cold-blooded? *(page 22)*
16. **Where do** emerald tree boas live? *(page 23)*
17. **What is the difference** between turtles and tortoises? *(page 24)*
18. **Where do giant** tortoises live? *(page 25)*
19. **What is a female** peafowl called? *(page 26)*
20. **Which bird** takes its name from its beautiful woven nest? *(page 27)*
21. **What do we call birds** that hunt animals for food? *(page 28)*

22. **Which is** the fastest bird? *(page 29)*
23. **What do** penguins eat? *(page 30)*
24. **Which are the largest** and the smallest penguins? *(page 31)*
25. **How do tree frogs** grip branches? *(page 32)*
26. **What are the main differences** between frogs and toads? *(page 33)*
27. **What do fish** use to breathe? *(page 34)*
28. **How do electric eels** catch their prey? *(page 35)*
29. **What happens to sharks** if they stop swimming? *(page 36)*
30. **Which is the world's** smallest shark? *(page 37)*
31. **What are the three** main parts of an insect's body? *(page 38)*
32. **What kind of insect** is a ladybird? *(page 39)*
33. **In the life cycle of a butterfly,** which stage comes after the caterpillar? *(page 40)*
34. **How are butterflies and moths different** when they rest? *(page 41)*
35. **How do garden spiders** catch insects? *(page 42)*
36. **How many legs** does a spider have? *(page 43)*
37. **Which crab steals its home** from other sea creatures? *(page 44)*
38. **Is it true** that most crabs walk sideways? *(page 45)*

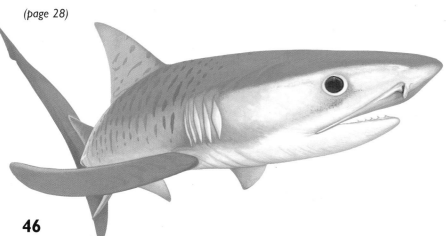

Index

ACKNOWLEDGMENTS

The publishers wish to thank the following artists who have contributed
to this book:

Terry Riley p9 (TR), p11 (C), p12 (C), p13 (T), p14 (C), p14-15(C), p18(B), p25
(CR), p26 (CL), p30 (C), p32 (B), p33 (BL);
Gillian Platt (Illustration Ltd.) p8 (CL), p9 (BL), p19 (B), p31 (C),
p33 (R), p42 (C), p43 (C);
Mike Foster (The Maltings Partnership) p13 (CR), p15, p19 (CR), p21 (TR),
p29 (C), p33 (CL), p39 (BL), p44 (TL);
Martin Camm p16-17 (B), p17 (TR), p21 (CR), p23 (CL), p24 (BR), p27 (CL),
p29 (TC, CR), p36 (T), p37 (C), p45 (TL, CL);
Michael Woods p19 (CL), p20 (B), p26 (CR), p28 (BL), p29 (CL), p36 (B), p38
(TL), p40 (CR), p41 (C);
Michael White (Temple Rogers) p38 (BR);
Roger Stewart p 37 (TR).

The publishers wish to thank the following for supplying photographs for this
book:

Miles Kelly archives p8 (BL, TR, CR), p9 (TL, MR), p10 (TL, B), p11 (T, CL, CR),
p12 (TL, BL, TR), p13 (BL), p14 (TL, TR), p15 (TL, CL, TR), p16 (CL, TR), p17 (CL,
CR), p18 (TR), p19 (TR), p20 (TL, BR), p21 (TL), p22 (TL, BL), p23 (TR, B), p24
(TR, BL), p25 (TL, BL), p26 (TR, B), p27 (T, TL, TR, C, BL, BR), p28 (TL), p29 (TL,
B), p30 (TL, TR, CB), p31 (TR), p32 (TL, CR), p33 (TL), p34 (CL, BR, TR), p35 (TL,
BR, C, TR), p37 (TR, BR), p39 (BL), p39 (TL, C, CL), p40 (CL, BR, TR), p41 (CL, C,
TR, CR), p42 (TR, TL, CR, BL), p43 (BL, CR, TR), p44 (TR,, BL, CR), p45 (TR, CR)
All model photography by **Mike Perry at David Lipson Photography Ltd.**

Models in this series:

Lisa Anness, Sophie Clark, Alison Cobb, Edward Delaney, Elizabeth Fallas, Ryan
French, Luke Gilder, Lauren May Headley, Christie Hooper, Caroline Kelly, Alice
McGhee, Daniel Melling, Ryan Ouyeyemi, Aaron Phipps, Eriko Sato, Jack Wallace.

Clothes for model photography supplied by:
Adams Children's Wear.